Circular Saws by Humbert Wolfe

Humbert Wolfe CB CBE was born on 5th January 1885 in Milan, Italy from Jewish family roots.

Wolfe was brought up in Bradford, West Yorkshire and was a pupil at Bradford Grammar School before attending Wadham College at the University of Oxford.

Beginning at the Board of Trade and then the Ministry of Labour, Wolfe's career was in the Civil Service, where he achieved positions of high responsibility.

He was also one of the most popular and prolific authors of the 1920's and 30s across some 40 works, mainly poetry but including other genres. Indeed, Gustav Holst set a number of his verses to song in his 12 Humbert Wolfe Songs, Op. 48 (1929).

In 1931 he became a Fellow of Royal Society of Literature and was one of the favourites to become the next Poet Laureate where he was up against Rudyard Kipling, W.B.Yeats and the eventual occupant-to-be of the post Robert Bridges. Wolfe was also a noted translator including that of Heinrich Heine, Edmond Fleg and Eugene Heltai (Heltai Jenő).

In 1938 Wolfe was appointed Deputy Secretary to the Ministry of Labour and his main responsibility was to equip the country's labour force for the approaching Second World War. His duties then extended to drawing up a list of writers who could better serve as propagandists rather than soldiers in the British Army.

Although Wolfe was married, he engaged in a decade long affair with the novelist Pamela Frankau which ended only with his death.

Humbert Wolfe CB CBE died on 5th January 1940 at 75 Eccleston Square in London. It was his 55th birthday.

Index of Contents

!

WASTE NOT, WANT NOT

When Haroun-al-Raschid (of whom I have told you before, and if I haven't it is only because I have forgotten) was having a bath they wouldn't let him splash. "By the beard of Allah," he observed mildly to the Vizier, who was standing by with his favourite celluloid duck (guaranteed to float), "this is preposterous. Cannot the Commander of the Faithful splash a little water? What's the good of being a King, that's what I say?" "Sire," replied the Vizier, handing him the celluloid duck, "the higher, the fewer the pleasures of life. And remember in season the saying, 'Waste not, want not.'"

The following day torrential rains of unprecedented severity visited Bagdad, sweeping away houses and gardens and drowning, among others, in circumstances of peculiar discomfort, the Grand Vizier. "Well," said Haroun, splashing in his bath (and hitting the opposite wall, mind you), "that only shows."

LOOKING FOR A NEEDLE IN A HAYSTACK

Mr. Arthur Benacres—the celebrated philanthropist—suffered in private life the inconvenience of being an ostrich. This was due to the act of a rather deaf fairy friend of the family, who mistook an observation on the weather (addressed to him by a conversational curate at the christening) for a request for feathers.

This, as you suppose, caused Mr. Benacres some difficulty, and led him to consider methods of escape. For though it was agreeable to be able to subsist on odd scraps of broken rubbish, and to dig with his head (instead of a spade) in the nice clean sand, people did make a fuss on the Underground and at parties.

Till at last another fairy friend of the family, who was neither deaf or blind, said: "Why don't you go into Parliament? Then nobody will notice." And they didn't.

ALL'S WELL THAT ENDS WELL

Once upon a time there was a princess whose mother would not buy her an umbrella. This was due to the wicked incompetence of the Prime Minister of that country, who, having no children of his own, spent all his money on swords instead of umbrellas. (Yes, I know swords are nicer generally, but these weren't; besides they were two-edged.) Moreover, her mother went and bought her a most unbecoming mackintosh—the sort that cuts your chin. And so, as it was raining all the time (for this princess lived at Kilcreggan in Dumbartonshire), she asked to be turned into a frog or a toad, because they didn't need umbrellas, and their mackintoshes fit at the neck.

Well, she was, and then she found that being a frog she couldn't use her scooter, or read "Antony and Cleopatra" to her mother, or go into Kensington Gardens with her father. (No! Kensington Gardens isn't at Kilcreggan, but this is a fairy princess, and so it doesn't matter.) So she unwished herself, and she was a princess, and she had no umbrella and a mackintosh that didn't fit at the neck. But it was a drought.[A] So all's well that ends well.

[A] A drought is when it doesn't rain at all. The scene of the story has been shifted from Scotland.

FAINT HEART NEVER WON FAIR LADY

Miss June Mortifex was most beautiful—yes, and more beautiful than that. So that when she looked out of the window the Meteorological Department in Exhibition Road, Kensington, over the Post Office, said:

"The westerly depression over London is now moving rapidly northward with a southern twist," which means nothing, and only shows how excited they all were.

But on account of her very exceptional beauty everybody was afraid of marrying her because they said "She would cost a King's Hansom," and owing to the increase in the number of motor taxicabs nobody had one about them.

So one day she blacked her face and assuming a Mid-Victorian Cockney accent went down Piccadilly singing the well-known ditty:

"O Mr. Jansen,
You kissed me in the hansom,
'Ansom is as 'ansom does,
Now you push me off the bus."

As may be supposed, this remarkable revival aroused the interest of a distinguished literary critic, who, recognising merit, even under an unpromising exterior, offered his hand, shortly after followed by his heart. "But, Edward," whispered June, "I am not what I seem." "You couldn't be," he answered triumphantly, "the Victorians never were."

And with that he walked into St. George's, Hanover Square, and ordered three of the best banns they had. And he gave her as a bridal gift the collected works of Mr. Edmund Gosse, for he was not faint-hearted.

V

TRUTH IS STRANGER THAN FICTION

It's no good pretending that Petronella Gibbs was a good princess. For one thing, she was always asking questions. And if the nurses didn't know the answer they were instantly beheaded. With the result that there was an unprecedented shortage in the supply of domestic labour. The Queen, her mother, indeed remarked to a friend of hers, another Queen living in the palace opposite, that "she never." You may suppose therefore that things had reached a crisis.

But did Petronella care? She did not care. She could do without nurses, thank you. On the contrary, she decided to start answering questions. For instance. For a long time all the best people had wanted to know "Who's Who." And a very large and important book had been written about it. Petronella wrote as follows:

"Deer Editter.
Nobody is.
Yours evva,
Petronella P."

This, which was the obvious solution, created considerable consternation. The Queen—her mother—had a long consultation with the King—her father—on his return from the Royal Exchange, where he kept his bulls, bears and hyenas, and remarked, "I never." But the King only laughed. That is why so many women are Republicans.

At last Petronella became so celebrated that the King of America, colloquially known as the President of the United States, asked for her hand in marriage. He and his subjects had been guessing so long that they thought that the time had come to find someone who knew.

The flattering offer was accepted by her royal parents, and Petronella, with great pomp and ceremony, embarked. Upon her arrival she was met by the leading citizens, who asked her, "What do you think of America?" "I don't," she replied, which was the right answer. At which they, being accustomed to the latter, and never previously having met the former, exclaimed, "Truth is stranger than fiction," and adding, "not half so true either," asked her with tears in their eyes to return where they asserted she belonged. Which she did. And both she and the King of America lived happily ever after.

VI

A ROSE BY ANY OTHER NAME WOULD SMELL AS SWEET

When Arthur Nobbs was a little boy he believed in fairies. If, for example, he ate part of his sister's jam (as he constantly did), he assured her that the fairies would put it back. And if they didn't, well that was because she didn't believe in them.

When he grew older and became a business man he naturally continued to entertain that belief. When he was successful (as he generally was) in his business transactions, he ascribed his success to the fairies, though the persons he so continuously and cleverly ruined thought that he had got the name wrong.

One day he met a starving sculptor whose father he had been able to put out of business. "What are these horrible objects that you have in your tray?" he asked severely. "These," said the sculptor, "are the seven fairies in which you believe." "But," objected Mr. Nobbs, "they are labelled 'The Seven Deadly Sins,' and they look it." "Oh," said the sculptor, "the title is only a matter of taste." "You are an impostor, sir," exclaimed Mr. Nobbs; "but fortunately we are in a law-abiding country." And he gave the young man in charge for seeking to obtain money by false pretences.

But you will be glad to learn that Arthur Nobbs was subsequently raised to the peerage and died universally beloved and respected, and on his tombstone they carved the simple phrase:

"He believed in fairies."

VII

A LITTLE KNOWLEDGE IS A DANGEROUS THING

The father of Miss Liddell was favourably known to the general public as the man who had written to the public prints during a strike a bold letter beginning: "Sir,—Let all strikers be shot. Then let ..." and again during a lock-out an equally bold letter with the following introduction: "Sir,—Let all employers be shot. Then let ..." (It is believed that it is from this use of "let" in public correspondence that the word "letter" is derived.)

Miss Liddell, therefore, naturally objected to the fact that the Prince, over whose education she presided, disliked the manly game of football. "Don't you know," she would say from time to time, "what Wellington said about the playing fields of Eton?" "No," the Prince used to reply, "who was Wellington? One of those professional footballers one reads about in their newspapers?" "Certainly not," Miss Liddell was wont to reply. "He was a great general who beat the French." "What did he do that for?" the Prince would ask. "Because they were his country's enemies." "Ah!" the Prince would say, "but I thought the French were England's friends." "So they are now," Miss Liddell would say. "And did Wellington beat them because of football?" the Prince would inquire. "Wellington said so," Miss Liddell (slightly flushed) would reply.

"Will you give me my paint-box?" the Prince would murmur politely.

VIII

TWO WRONGS DO NOT MAKE A RIGHT

Listen. This is quite a new story. It is about a swan that wished he was an ugly duckling again. He was one of those two swans who stand at the edge of the Round Pond, have black feet and holes to put tape through in their beaks. Only they won't let you put tape through.

What he said was (quite simply), "Liberty, Equality and Fraternity." To which his mate said, "Then why do you always eat more than your share?" But the other swan was an idealist and took no notice.

He summoned a public meeting of the ducks after closing-time, and having elected himself to the chair after rather a protracted argument with a pertinacious old drake, told his audience that he was a duck at heart. "What is beauty," he went on to say, "that it should put one on a lonely eminence. The exquisite shape of the swan, his girl-like neck, what right to rule do these confer?" "None," said the old drake, heartily. "Did you say beauty?" said a young female duck, bridling her feathers. "Why you poor old antic, if you knew how we ducks sympathised with you on your deformity!"

But this was a little too much for the swan. "I did not come here to be insulted," he said hotly, "by a brood of blasphemous pond-puddlers. Are you aware that the Great Swan made swans in his image?" "And are you aware," said the old drake, "that the swans retorted by making him in theirs?"

"Well," said his mate to the rather draggled swan who returned about midnight, "how did you get on?" "Get on," he screamed, "those ducks think that equality means that I'm equal with them." "And doesn't it?" "Certainly not," said the swan, tucking his head under his wings, "it means that they're equal with me." "And what's more," he said with sudden truculence as he emerged for a moment, "a swan's a swan for a' that."

BUSINESS IS BUSINESS

The electric bell had rung for the fourth time, when the door was opened by an agreeable young man dressed in the height of fashion.

"Who are you?" he inquired in the amiable tone of one who begins an interesting conversation.

"I'm the Milk," retorted the young man with the cans a little shortly, for he was not pleased at being so long delayed.

"Will you not come in one moment?" the young householder retorted. "I have within the butcher, the grocer and the baker, and I have long desired to add you to the list of my visitors."

The young milkman (still carrying his heavy can) followed the polite young gentleman into a fine, lofty room. The whole was arranged with exquisite taste, and many deep rugs indicated a luxurious vein in the young man's character. At the further end of the room, arranged neatly in an isosceles triangle (for the baker was much shorter than the other two), were the corpses of the butcher, the baker, and the grocer.

"May I inquire," said the Milk, after surveying the scene in silence for a minute, "why you have killed these three gentlemen?"

"You have the best of rights in the world to ask, and I shall be delighted to explain," answered the young gentleman courteously. "You must know, then, that I have a speculative interest in the manner in which the smaller British tradesman meets death. I have been much charmed by the experience I have gleaned with the help of my three friends there. The butcher," he added, pointing smilingly to a discolouration on his forehead, "was the least graceful. And now as I have answered you, perhaps you will allow me to ask you a question?"

"But pray do," answered the Milk, not to be outdone in courtesy.

"I thank you. I was going to inquire whether you knew any reason why I should not add you to my list."

"I apprehended," returned the Milk, "that your question might be something of that sort. I had gone so far as to prepare an answering question."

"And what might that be?" inquired the young gentleman?

"Why should I not kill you?" retorted the Milk affably.

"There is something in what you say," exclaimed the young gentleman. "I had not considered the question. Will you give me a minute or two to meditate?"

"I must be about my business, I am afraid," returned the Milk, quietly bludgeoning the young man as he spoke with his milk can. "Yet how sad it is," he said reflectively surveying the four corpses, "that speculation must inevitably make way for practical affairs."

And with that he proceeded to replace the milk he had spilled with water from a neighbouring table.

X

LET SLEEPING DOGS LIE

Once upon a time there was a wizard who could find the truth in a newspaper.

Fortunately he was discovered and hanged in time, and since then nobody has dared to tamper with the liberty of the Press.

XI

IT'S NEVER TOO LATE TO MEND

North of Skellefteå, in the kingdom of Sweden, there lived a more than usually repulsive troll, who was, however, the supreme Scandinavian authority on psycho-analysis. The pine-trees in that part of the world walk down to the water of the sea as though the weight of their own beauty had become too heavy for them. And the sea with blandishing whispers holds out to them the immense temptation of his cold peace.

On a rock at the rendezvous of sea and pines, under a midnight-sun-haunted sky of June, the troll sat with huge horn glasses on his twisted nose relentlessly reading the work which Mr. Freud was to write some centuries later....

Out of the shadows of the pine, as straight, as serious, and weighed down like them with the burden of her own loveliness, slipped the Princess Gurli on her way to the cold temptation of the sea. Like other princesses before and after, she was enchanted. When she looked at her almost flawless loveliness in the lily-pond of her father's castle, she saw always a faint silver mist that trembled at her mirrored lips. The mist would draw together into a frangible bubble, a diaphanous ball of silver, and finally dissolve, leaving an infinite argent stain on the red of her mouth.

One day a fish had swum up from the marble floor, and rising to the surface, had said to her, "What will you give me if I drink the mist?" And she had answered, "What do you wish?" "Your soul," he replied. This she was glad in any case to be rid of, for her soul had often interfered with the natural pleasures to which she was entitled by her loveliness.

The fish and the mist disappeared together, and for the first time she saw herself in flawless loveliness. But she was strangely cold.

Princes came to her from the North and the South, but when they looked into the green stain of her eyes they shivered and turned away. The Princess was not sorry, for she thought that men were a poor substitute for her own beauty. But with her twenty-first summer she was conscious that her beauty was threatened. For a neighbouring queen had been heard to say of her, "Yes, she is lovely. But for me her beauty has no soul."

Therefore she decided to marry a prince of her own choice, who would ask all of her and nothing, whose castle has no lamps and whose palace gardens are visited neither by sun nor snow.

It was on her way to this alliance that she slipped out of the pines, and beheld on the rock under the midnight-sun-haunted sky the unusually repulsive troll reading the prenatal works of Mr. Freud.

"Ha," neighed the troll, looking up, "you have come to consult me, Princess Gurli." "I have not," said the Princess. "I do not like trolls." "But I," said the troll, "am not like other trolls." "That is what all trolls say," replied the Princess scornfully. "Perhaps," said the troll, "but I am the greatest Scandinavian authority on psycho-analysis!" "What in Valhalla," said the Princess, "is that?" "The study of souls," cried the troll with a significant chuckle. "Oh," said the Princess, "you can't study mine. I haven't got one." "This is interesting," said the troll; "you are undoubtedly suffering from an advanced condition of mermaid-complex." "What does that mean?" said the Princess. "It means that you have a suppressed passion for a Mer-King," replied the troll, "and if you give way to it you will be cured immediately." "I have never heard anything so disgusting," said the Princess. "Why, a Mer-King is half a fish." "Half a fish," said the troll sententiously, "is better than no fish." "I had meant," said the Princess, "to drown myself in the sea because the loss of my soul troubled me. But now that I know that souls are things that can be studied by creatures like you, I am very glad I have not got one."

The troll was so shocked at this outburst that he fell backwards into the sea, where he was instantly seized by mermaids and drowned. But the Princess went back, slim and gold, through the shadow of the pines, and married the youngest son of the nearest fishmonger.

XII

ARS LONGA, VITA BREVIS

At about half-past eleven on a summer evening there might have been observed, wending her way slowly along the Rue du Soleil Levant into the Cour de St. Pierre at Geneva, a small black kitten with her tail straight up. There was nobody in the cobbled square except the beech-tree in the middle with a wooden seat round him. The kitten, who was being brought up on a severely anti-religious basis, doubted whether the tree might not have been influenced by the cathedral window, in whose shadow he had dreamed summer and winter for more than a hundred years. She was therefore on the point of slipping into a most engaging gutter of stone, like a deep mouse-track, that leads past the chapel of Calvin to the railings that overlook the Passage des Degrés des Poules.

But the beech wasn't going to stand that. On the contrary! He dropped one little fidgety brown leaf— puff!—between the kitten's paws, who, throwing religious prejudice to the winds, played with it as enchantingly as though it had been a convert to Epistemological Radicalism.

Then the moon looked over the crooked gables into the square, and proceeded to light her cold lamp in all the dark cathedral windows. But the beech rustled her leaves warningly at her. "What is it?" said the moon, and then she saw the little black kitten dancing with the leaf on the cobbles. "Who is your little black faun of a friend?" she inquired of the beech. "I don't know her name," said the beech, "but she certainly dances extremely well."

At this point the kitten stopped abruptly and said a little harshly, "What are you two old ones whispering about?" "We were remembering," said the beech, who was a kindly old fellow, "the time when we also danced with our shadows in the joy of our youth." "How can that be?" said the kitten impatiently. "The moon never was young, and you never had but one leg, and that stuck in the ground. You are telling me fairy tales, and I have no patience with them. Let me tell you my dancing is merely automatic muscular reaction." "Dear me," said the moon mildly, "what long words that child uses! But tell me, little one, if you don't like fairy tales, you won't want to hear the story of the cat and the fiddle." "Does it observe the dramatic unities?" inquired the kitten. "I don't know what they are," said the moon, "but it has a moral." "Which is more than you have, you little wretch," said the beech severely. "Oh well," said the kitten ungraciously, "I suppose I must hear it, though I expect that it will be representational."

"Once upon a time," said the moon, "there was a cat that had the soul of a musician. But when she tried to render her thoughts into sound she excited no sympathetic response. On the contrary, people threw boots and bottles at her. 'I do not care,' said the cat, 'my songs are for posterity.' But nevertheless the constant succession of missiles disturbed her."

"It is my considered opinion," interrupted the kitten, "that she was no artist. The best art rejects appreciation."

"So the dog said," observed the moon, "when he was chasing the cat up the tree with yells of derision. But the cat was not comforted.

"Finally one day as she wandered disconsolate through a field she met a very tragic cow lowing, as it seemed to the cat, with a mild haunting beauty. When she came up with the cow the cat observed that her eyes were streaming with tears. 'How is it,' said the cat, 'that you who are notoriously as unmusical as a milk-can can low with a beauty that brings tears to your own eyes.' 'It is not my music that brings tears to my eyes, but my lost calf. And let me tell you, cat, that till you also play on the strings of your own heart you will never make music.'"

"This is very affecting," said the beech-tree; "and very untrue," added the kitten.

"The cat resolved this dark saying till one day she heard in the dining-room the delicate symphony of a spoon upon a china plate. Presently the sound ceased and the cat jumped upon the table to investigate. 'How is it,' said she to the empty dish, 'that you make such exquisite music though you are nothing but baked clay?' 'It is the loss of the beautiful jelly that adorned me that sings,' said the dish, 'and let me tell you, cat, that till you also play upon the strings of your own heart you will never make music.'

"'This is very strange,' thought the cat, but she continued nevertheless to sing as before without sympathetic response. Till at last an angry old gentleman obtained a gun and shot the cat dead."

"This story is in very bad taste," said the kitten.

"I think she richly deserved it," said the beech.

"Wait a minute," said the moon, "the story is not finished. An old poor maker of fiddle-strings found the cat on his way home. And about a month later a young fiddler of the country called upon him to buy some strings. 'These are the best I have ever made,' said the old man. That night," went on the moon, "the fiddler played under a window of a high house in the Place de la Taconnerie an old German tune, 'Einst o wunder.' And now no one threw boots and missiles, but out of a high lattice fell a white rose."

"That is a very beautiful story," said the beech, "and now I am almost sorry for the cat." "You need not be," said the moon; "even if her life was short her art"—"was in the right place," rudely interjected the impertinent kitten. "But what I want to know is, who shot the fiddler?" "I am afraid," replied the moon, "that I must be going about my business."

XIII

SUNT CERTI DENIQUE FINES

"What will the next story be about?" said the publisher. "I'm not sure that I shall publish the book at all if it's about Swedish trolls and Genevese cats. Couldn't you write about something British—a gnome who made 94 not out for Surrey and then went home and drank a bottle of stout?" "I not only can," said the author, "but I immediately will."

"There was once," said the author, "a sprite who thought goloshes and hot water bottles unmanly. He preferred east winds and colds in the head, and being strong and silent (though he sneezed a good deal from time to time), and though he was a pagan himself, he could respect Christianity in others. His name was Puck; he lived at Bexhill."

"I have been expecting this for some time," broke in the publisher; "all you do is to take other people's noble conceptions and distort them. Disguising plagiarism as travesty, you seek to impose on the public. But let me tell you, sir, in the words of the Latin poet, 'Sunt certi denique fines.'"

"I am sorry to have given offence," said the author, "particularly as I would have wished to sketch a new version of Puck's life, when as a result of continued exposure to draughts in what the Americans taught him to call God's Great Out-at-Elbows he contracted a vivid form of rheumatism. So crippled, he devoted his declining years to Worthing and the pleasures of a bath chair. Not unnaturally in these circumstances he developed a horror of Sussex and of children, and found his only remaining happiness in reading the poems of Mr. Edward Shanks to the local clergy. When he died, as he did shortly after this—"

"I am only surprised," interrupted the publisher bitterly, "that the clergy survived."

"Oh," said the author, "they did not survive long. It is true that their counsel at the trial urged that it was justifiable homicide in self-defence, but the judge quite properly pointed out in his summing-up that they needn't have listened. But I can see," went on the author, "that this is not the sort of story of which you were in need. Let me therefore recount to you the true story of Jack and the Beanstalk."

"I hope that it is not very long," said the publisher.

"That depends on the method of payment," replied the author. "If I am paid by the word, of course—"

"Get on with the story," said the publisher.

"By the side of a slow river in the western parts of a great metropolis there lived a boy named Jack. Though he was so young he was already justly celebrated for his climbing feats. Indeed, the old woman who looked after him was never tired of saying, with a roguish smile at herself in the mirror, 'C'est un vrai gosse!' which means in English, 'He takes after his spiritual grandmother.'

"Jack had climbed all the trees in his own garden and all those in everybody else's. And then one day he announced that he was going to climb an entirely new tree whose roots are in the heart but whose leaves are in eternity.... There was much discussion among his friends, some saying that he should climb and others that he shouldn't, and still others (but these were jealous) that it was little better than an Indian rope trick. But Jack was not to be deterred. For he said that he was tired of living among pygmies; he would now climb the Immortal Tree and slay one of the giants and return with his head.

"That night accordingly the tree was planted, and by morning its leaves hid the sky. After a farewell breakfast, at which a good deal of stout was drunk, and at which the Press was well represented, Jack started the ascent. He climbed up and up till he was out of sight. His friends waited about till nightfall, but as he did not return they concluded that he was making a night of it with the giants, and went home to their evening porter and bed.

"Next morning the tree was withered. Some said one thing and some said another. These, that the giants had insisted on Jack's remaining among them, and these (but these were traducers), that he had fallen to the first giant. The general view, however, was that Jack had burst with chagrin on discovering that, except for himself, there were no giants. But since his departure nobody has ever climbed the beanstalk, for, as they all said, 'Sunt certi denique fines.'"

"That story," said the publisher, "is worse than the first. That was vulgar, but this has no meaning whatever."

"You just publish it and see," said the author.

XIV

HEAVEN HELPS THOSE THAT HELP THEMSELVES

In the great days of Haroun-al-Raschid, when the minarets of Bagdad were sewn together against the sky like a gold embroidery on blue canvas, a certain merchant, whose name has unhappily not been preserved, was entering at nightfall with his camels and his asses through the Gold East Gate. The beggars, as was their custom, crowded round with shrill cries, extolling the merchant's virtues and their own miseries, and suggesting that the former might reasonably be expected to mitigate the latter. "In the name of the All-Compassionate, the All-Merciful," they murmured musically. But the merchant only wrapped his cloak round him closer, saying in a harsh voice, "Heaven helps those that help themselves."

At this moment one of the merchant's asses stumbled and beautiful red coins ran in the gutters under the pale yellow moon. With cries even more musical the beggars—not excluding those lame by profession—threw themselves upon the gold. "Sons of Shaitan," roared the merchant, "I will have you all strung up to the city gates by your toes and ears. I will have you flayed with red pepper. I will—"

"You surprise me, oh merchant," said a poet who had been a witness of the whole scene. "Is it no longer your view then that heaven helps those that help themselves?"

"Do you not see," screamed the merchant, "that it is an ass that helps them?" "Does that surprise you," inquired the poet, going on his way, "I gather from your appearance of wealth that heaven has already helped you."

XV

"YOU NEVER CAN TELL"

"This is a story for patriots," said the pin of the unexploded hand-grenade to the poppies among which he was rusting.

"What is a patriot?" asked the youngest of the poppies, who, I am afraid, was rather an affected puss and thought that the pin was in love with her.

"A patriot," said the pin, "is a man who loves his country so well that he dies for it."

"He would show his affection better to my mind," said a rather withered female poppy, "if he lived for it."

"Oh no," simpered the young poppy, "I think that death is so romantic."

"How adorable," sighed the hand-grenade, "are the enthusiasms of youth. I remember exactly the same innocent thrill when some five years ago I reposed among a pile of grenades like myself all going into action. We were doomed, we knew, to burst. But what did that matter? Our country called us."

"What country was that?" inquired one of the poppies.

"England," said the grenade proudly. "Bow, poppies, you are in the presence of a British bomb! It is true, of course, that my iron was dug in Spain, that my copper came from the New World, and that my explosives were in part foreign. But I was as pure British as anybody else."

"I'm sure you were," said the young poppy consolingly.

"When we came to the trench," continued the pin, "we were assigned each to a bomb-thrower. I myself fell to the lot of a young man beautiful as an angel and reckless as a devil. Grenade after grenade he tossed into the air with exquisite dexterity, and the frightful explosions and horrible cries that followed showed only too well how richly his skill had been rewarded. And now my great moment was at hand.

An attack was ordered. Over the parapet he leapt clasping me in his hand, and together we flew through the flying and screaming death about us. We reached the enemy trench. The loathsome horrors were actually attempting to shoot down our brave fellows. I am happy to say that the bayonet taught them better. But alas! I now come to the most awful moment in my life. We jumped into the trench. My hero raised his hand to throw me at one of the incarnate devils. And then—his hand dropped. 'Carl,' he whispered, 'is it you, Carl?' This, mind you, to an incarnate devil. 'George,' he replied, and though he was a devil, I confess his voice made me uneasy, 'has it come to this, dear brother? Throw the grenade. It will be better so. There can be no hell as foul as this.' 'What, murder you?' cried my ex-hero. 'Why not?' said the other wearily. 'After all, one more or one less, why should it matter to either of us?' 'I won't,' said George, 'not if they shoot me for it.' 'What?' said Carl, 'have you still a soul? Then by God I can die in peace.' And with that he shot himself through the heart. 'Kiss me, George,' he whispered, and George, dropping me as though I were of no account, kissed the crime-stained lips. And here in consequence I have been ever since."

"And what happened to George?" asked the oldest poppy. "Oh," said the grenade easily, "I am not sure. I heard—(and I hoped it was true) that he had been shot for cowardice in the face of the enemy."

"Would patriots like that story?" inquired the withered female poppy.

"Certainly," said the pin.

"Then," said the poppy, "you do not seem to me to make out a good case for patriots."

"Madam," said the grenade hotly, "you would not speak so if you were being threatened by the hobnailed boots of a gross invader, who was on the point of squashing you flat. Then you would be glad enough to have the protection of a patriot like myself." And the pin was so moved (and the sun so hot) that he suddenly and violently exploded, with the result that the poppies were scattered in fragments to the four winds of heaven.

XVI

UNITED WE STAND

Now listen! and if you can possibly avoid it don't interrupt. In the far and non-existent province of Arabia the population consisted almost exclusively of kings, except for the lower classes, who were, as everybody knows, emperors. The kings had it all their own way for years and years, when suddenly the emperors formed a trade society, popularly known as the Amalgamated Emperors' Union. In pursuance of the principle upon which all such societies rest (in non-existent provinces), the emperors, as a preliminary step, ceased the function which distinguished their calling. The kings were thereupon compelled to act both as kings and emperors, which caused them inconvenience. Accordingly they summoned a special meeting of Sanhedrim—the Arabian legislative assembly—and passed a law withdrawing the right of association among emperors (though naturally preserving it for kings), and severely forbidding, under penalty, what was described in the Act as "striking."

In Arabia—that fabulous country—a law on being duly passed by the kings becomes automatically a law of nature. So that it is very necessary to pay the greatest attention to the drafting. On this occasion the framers of the Bill had forgotten by an unaccountable oversight to omit "clocks" from the exclusion clause. In consequence all clocks in the province automatically ceased striking, and thereafter it was no use consulting an Arabian constable because nobody in that legendary land knew what o'clock it was.

"I suppose," said the publisher scornfully, "you think that's clever and Socialistic, and all that sort of thing. Have you any idea what wages we have to pay to the book-binders?"

"I asked you not to interrupt," said the author. "Now you've prevented me from explaining how the clock in the principal mosque—"

"I don't believe they have clocks in mosques," said the publisher.

" how the clock in the principal mosque welcomed the change, observing that it for one had always been in favour of methods of conciliation. 'And anyhow,' the church clock continued as it finally ran down, 'why bother about time when you have eternity?'"

"Have you any aspirin?" inquired the publisher.

XVII

ICI-GÎT

When at creation God was faced With earth's illimitable waste, We understand that what he said is: "Let there be light,"—and there was Geddes.

XVIII

SILENCE IS GOLDEN

"You will observe," remarked the placid convict, negligently dropping his pick on the warder's foot, "that a very few words express a great deal."

The warder, who had already expressed more than a little in his first two words, stopped abruptly, and with a graceful wave of his hand bade the convict be seated. "For this," he added, "is a subject to which I have devoted much thought, and you with your varied experience of men and manners should speak with authority."

"It is true," admitted the convict agreeably, "that in the course of the commission of a certain number of tolerably execrable crimes I have been brought into contact with many people, but I have made it a rule never to allow my conversation to be affected by the practical affairs of life. To be personal is to be dull without redemption."

"But in your case," interrupted the warder, "your experiences are so unusual that you might well be forgiven for dwelling on them."

"That," retorted the felon, with a certain graceful melancholy, "is the conviction of every conversationalist. But I have never supposed that a murder was necessarily interesting just because I had perpetrated it."

"This sort of trait," murmured the custodian of the condemned, "elicits a man's respect. But," he continued aloud, "what, then, is left us to discuss?"

"The universe," smilingly returned the convict, "and any other fictions you may care to invent. The whole world loves a liar. I admit," he added, with a gentle shrug, "that 'Not guilty' was an error, but that you will understand was more by way of repartee than of continuous conversation. The judge, after all, drew the retort on himself."

"But truth, I have always understood, is stranger—"

"Pardon me if I interrupt," said the criminal a little sternly, "but I cannot stand by and hear a friend (for I include you in that number)," he added courteously enough, "quote proverbs. I can forgive your being a warder of condemned men, but I cannot stand your being a guardian of (forgive me!) damned phrases."

"You hold, then," returned the warder, a little confused, "that quotation is not admissible in polite conversation."

"You cannot quote a proverb," earnestly responded the prisoner, "any more than you can butter a hypothesis. But I perceive," he went on more gently, "that I have fallen into the fault of heat. Forgive a hotheadedness which has more than once ruined my conversation."

"But I have nothing to forgive," cried the custodian, much affected. "It is I who am the more to blame."

"That, indeed, is true," interjected the Governor of the gaol, who had come up unobserved during the latter part of the conversation, "and, much as I shall regret your loss, I must reconcile myself to it. While you," he went on, turning to the convict, "will have leisure, when consuming bread and water, to reflect whether, after all, there is not something to be said for silence."

XIX

LOOK BEFORE YOU LEAP: OR, REFLECTIONS BEFORE YOU JUMP

"I am tired of reflection," said the looking-glass, "I will now live my own life." As a first step to that end he succeeded in rolling himself right out of his seventeenth-century uprights and falling off the spindle-legged dressing-table, oval face downwards, on to a deep grey carpet.

"Dear me," said the carpet, who was rather a simple old-fashioned thing, though of an excellent texture, "here is somebody come down in the world. Ahem! I hope, sir, that you are none the worse for your fall."

"Certainly not," replied the mirror, who was rather bewildered by the fall and the complete darkness in which his new situation had placed him, "I precipitated myself to the ground on purpose." "What!" cried the carpet, who feared that she had to do with a self-murderer, "after full reflection?"

"Without any reflection whatever," cried the mirror testily. "I am," he added more suavely, "entirely incapable of such an act."

"Poor thing," said the carpet soothingly, for she now perceived that her affair was merely with a madman. "If you will only compose yourself I am sure you will be your own man again immediately."

"I see, madam," said the mirror, "that we do not understand each other. Let me therefore explain my point of view. You must know then that I am by nature a person of a profoundly original turn of thought. Judge then of my despair when a malignant fate ordained for more than a century that I should be tortured by serving merely to reflect the follies and lack of grace of others. I have borne things insupportable, and finally I took the magnificent decision which has, among, other agreeable circumstances of release, conferred upon me the pleasure of your conversation. You will conceive for yourself my mental tumult when you used the word 'reflection.'"

"But, sir," said the carpet, now much distressed, "reflect. Are you not flying in the face of Providence? If reflection was the gift bestowed upon you by your designer would you wantonly dissipate it? Such conduct, believe me, must have the most dire results!"

"Madam," neighed the mirror with an accent that suggested his century, "I am, I hope, a mirror of Feeling, and I know what respect must ever be paid to the Fair. None the less, I cannot leave you a prey to common error, even though its removal should offend your Female Delicacy. M'am, there is no such thing as a designer, but each of us is his own architect."

"No designer!" screamed the carpet. "Now the weaver be good to me! Impious creature, do you not know that we are each of us made with nicely adjusted virtues and qualities by an all-understanding maker? And that to doubt this is to be damned beyond hope of re-weaving?"

"And what, m'am," sneered the mirror, "is your particular virtue?"

"To be a comfort and a support to the foot, an office of which I am proud," replied the carpet.

"I dare swear," said the mirror courteously, "that you are perfect in it. But I do not doubt that, were I called upon, I could adjust myself to the same task in spite of all the pretensions of your friend the designer."

The carpet was spared the necessity of continuing so sacrilegious a conversation by the entry into the darkened room of its owner. He stepped heavily in the direction of the dressing-table, and stamped his riding-boot hard on the back of the mirror, smashing the glass to fragments.

"Damn!" he cried loudly, and after switching on the lights rang for a servant. "Who has been so d—d clumsy as to leave the old mirror standing between the window and the door?"

The servant picked up the mirror. "I'm sorry, sir," he said, "but it's only the glass as is smashed. We could easy get a new one put in, and you were always complaining that the old one didn't reflect."

"Very well," said the owner, "but the glass must be put right. Tell them to let me see the designer before the work is begun—and sweep up the litter of glass. By the way, the carpet's not injured, is it?"

"No, sir," said the servant, busily sweeping, "the carpet's perfectly all right."

XX

LIBERTY, EQUALITY, FRATERNITY

"There is a good deal of talk in certain circles," said the deuce of spades casually to the ace of hearts, "as to the need for equality among cards."

"And how," inquired the ace amicably, "is this equality to be established?"

"There are three schools of thought," replied the deuce readily; "the first holds that all cards should rank as deuce, while the second that all should be aces. I myself have ventured to favour a golden mean of all counting, say, as nine."

"There is a great deal in all these theories," replied the ace, "and I think one or other should be immediately adopted. There is, however, one point on which I should like to sound a note of caution. I do not quite see how in the altered circumstances any game is to be played."

"Oh, we have thought of that," said the deuce carelessly, "and frankly we do not see the necessity of the game."

"Then," said the ace, "I have nothing more to say."

XXI

QUIS SEPARABIT?

Two statesmen of well-merited celebrity in their own countries and times, having for a moment escaped the vigilance of their warders, met in a comparatively cool corner of hell to discuss the possibility of forming a new government.

"I do not feel," said the first, "that H.H. any longer really represents the feeling in the circles."

"I entirely agree," said the second; "he is still, I fear, a hopeless reactionary and continues to believe that there is a distinction between evil and good—a doctrine which all advanced thought has long since abandoned."

"And not only that," said the first, "he is still a prey to the war spirit. He is for ever thinking in terms of the great conflict in which he thinks he was defeated. As a matter of fact, if he could only realise the truth, heaven was by far the greater sufferer, and is greatly embarrassed by the reparation exacted from him."

"There is only one way," said the second, "to repair the ravages of that unfortunate misunderstanding, and that is to recognise frankly that heaven and hell are necessary to one another and to arrange for a policy of goodwill and intercelestial understanding."

"Nor should we stop at that," replied the first, taking fire, as well he might, at the enunciation of sentiments so lofty; "mere understanding is not enough. We must have a pact, co-operation, even coalition."

"With a common policy," broke in the second, "resting on the best of evil and the worst of good."

"The only difficulty," said the first, "that I can see is one of the leadership."

"We must not," replied the second, "permit these wretched personalities to interfere with policies of universal benefit. Moreover, I am sure that the two forces are both too large-minded to let their personal inclinations stand in the way. And in any case, is it not possible that as a result of this great movement they may come to realise—"

"Yes," cried the first breathlessly.

"—that they themselves are one and the same personality?"

XXII

MEN, NOT MEASURES

"What is that little man with the soul like a wet umbrella, that somebody has left in a corner, doing?" inquired the lovely, though scarcely visible, presence that had unexpectedly materialised the night before in the house of the Prime Minister of Samaria.

"Hush," whispered his conductor, the utterly outraged Private Secretary, "hush, they will hear you."

"Have no fear," said the radiant creature, looking carefully at the faces of the assembled Council, "my voice is of the kind that does not reach their ears. Therefore tell me what he is doing?"

"He is keeping minutes," said the Secretary, a little sullenly.

"Why does he do that?" inquired the angel. "Were I in his place I would shoo them on their way like a hen-yard full of hens."

"You do not understand," said the Secretary; "he is keeping a record of what is happening."

"But how does he know?" inquired the angel.

"By listening to what these gentlemen say," replied the Secretary.

"Dear me," said the angel, "if that is his only source of information I see that I must help him," and he walked across the Council chamber to the side of the luckless clerk, gently disregarding the frenzied gestures of the Private Secretary.

The Clerk had made the following entry in a neat flowing hand on a handsome sheet of thick white paper.

"The Prime Minister drew the Council's attention to the difficulties presented by the Poets' Birth (Prevention) Bill. The object, as his colleagues knew, was to secure that in future poets should be made (if possible by publicity) and not born. Everybody agreed that democracy should have self-made poets, that the pretensions of birth must cease. At the same time it could not be denied that poets insisted on being born. It would be within his colleagues' recollection that a number of poets had been made in the recent list of honours. They were, he was happy to say, perfect in every respect except that they did not write poetry. For his part he preferred that kind of poet, but it could not be denied that the opponents of the measure were making great play with this. He asked for the views of his colleagues.

"The Minister of Higher Education asked what poetry was?

"The Minister of Commerce entirely agreed.

"The Master of the Weasels thought that there was much in what had been said.

"The Senior Almoner had had a letter from a very respectable washerwoman in his constituency. She complained that there was a poet who wore soft collars. He did not wish to press the point, but popular feeling could not be neglected.

"The Keeper of the Conscience took the view that the time was ripe for action. Several members of the Council concurred.

"The Prime Minister, summing up, said that he was glad to find his colleagues unanimous in supporting the course he had proposed. The division was likely to be a close one. He especially appealed to Lord Albatross."

At this point the angel took possession of the Clerk's mind, and with a queer click the faces of the men round the table were rolled up like green railway carriage blinds, and their minds became visible, working rather like electric light studs being pressed off and on. The Clerk continued to write the minutes: "Not that Lord Albatross cared, but his stud would fidget his neck, and he couldn't be expected to listen to the Prime Minister's neat periods with a rasping stud. The other eighteen fellers probably had got their studs right. Anyhow, judgin' by their serious looks, they had better things than studs to think about. Queer thing how complete they all looked—if you know what I mean. Couldn't imagine them ever having not worn morning coats or neat grey tweeds and a sort of sewn-up-and-sent-home-hoping-it's-to-your-complete-satisfaction look. Except 'Conky,' the Lord High Wig. 'Conky' was dressed up like himself—a sort of suit consistin' of a heavy jowled face, glass eyes, looming stomach and the rest. Joke if they found him and 'Conky' out and gave them the push for having sneaked into the room during a Council." Albatross suppressed a chuckle.

The P.M. looked at him coldly. "Damn the fellow with his aristocratic sharpness. There he sat looking like a stuck pig, and all the time he had followed every word and seen through the whole caboodle. That's the worst of mixing classes. They've got their own cold, fishy way of nosing through the water, and snap—they're on the fly, when you thought them fast asleep. They'd never understand each other—never. Here was he not caring a row of beans (or has-beens, he added, viciously looking round) as to what the result of the division would be. What he wanted was friendship. He wanted them all to see that he wasn't just the best thing in talking machines that had been invented. Groping to them he was—to their hearts. Well, why not? They had hearts, hadn't they? And just when he was stretching out a hand to gather in the strings this cold fellow fetches out his knife of laughter. Not human, that's what was wrong. Born like a little Eastern idol. He should have stuck to his own lot. There was Crayfish, the Senior Almoner. He sympathised. He stood shoulder to shoulder. Damn! getting the rhetoric into his thoughts! Still Crayfish would pull it through, if only to irritate Albatross and Lord Conkers. If he didn't, well he'd get back to humans at last. He had a right, hadn't he, to be a man.

"The Minister of Commerce was drawing one O after another on his pad. Who did the perfect circle? Forget my own name next. Just ask old Crayfish—only chap in the room who's ever read anything except The Morning News—begging Albatross' pardon—and The Blue 'Un. Silly to have got cluttered up with this gang, and yet what a wonder the P.M. was. Never felt a thing in his life. Could make a bed—mattress and all—out of two adjectives and a noun. Yes, and the right adjectives too—right in a popular sense that is. But as a literary proposition, O Lord! How odd, though, to live by words that weren't words so much as gestures and nothing behind them. Like Hume association of well, not ideas, but penny plain dressed up as tuppeny coloured. Like a series of ballads hawked by a man in the street hung all round him and no man in the middle. Funny how not being a man he gets real men like old Crayfish for instance. That's the one—no rhetoric for him. Look at his tense simple eyes. He thinks only of what's best and loyalty, and if sincerity can get the damned thing through he'll do it. Now I wonder if he does know who did the perfect circle?..."

The blinds clicked down again. The Master of the Weasels was standing over the Clerk pouring some brandy down his throat. The Clerk blinked his eyes and recovered suddenly. "I'm sorry, sir, I must have fainted. I'm afraid that I've missed part of the discussion." "It doesn't matter," said the Prime Minister, looking at the notes, from which the angelic interpolations had disappeared. "Nobody said a thing while you were off." "Oh," said the Clerk happily, "then nothing happened. Will you sign the minutes?"

XXIII

YOU CANNOT HAVE YOUR CAKE AND EAT IT

A certain business-man in Damascus, whose efficiency was only surpassed by his personal ugliness, was informed that in a distant vilayet dwelt a peasant of whom it was currently rumoured that he possessed a goose that laid eggs of pure gold.

He accordingly chartered a caravan, and with much jingling of silver bells set out across the desert to make a proposition to the peasant. In his company was a young man who was reputed (though it had not been finally brought home to him) to be a poet. Whether this were true or no, it cannot be denied that he paid much heed to the ascensions of the moon.

On the third day of the pilgrimage that pale planet was bewitching in her pensive hair the reluctant black beauty of the desert. All was still except when a grave camel kneeling shook a bell. But presently, with the clear monotony of a bird, the young man's voice was heard singing:

"In this cold glory of midnight, day and her fever have passed away.

"Here in the quiet, here in the cool, even pain, even sorrow are beautiful.

"And the voice of the poet lifts and lingers at one in the dark with the older singers."

"As I feared," said the merchant, raising his head from his silken and tasselled pillow, "the fellow is a poet. I must cope with this." Thereupon he lifted the flap of his embroidered tent, and in a sleeping suit, of which the radiant texture did not conceal the irregular contours of his frame, with one arm behind his back, strode across the sand to where, in a patch of shadow, the poet was crooning.

"Young man," said the merchant, breaking somewhat harshly on the singer's reverie, "was that your own poem?"

"It was, merchant," replied the poet, "but now, since you have heard it, it is yours also."

"Tell me," said the merchant craftily, "how much would you be paid for such a poem in Damascus?"

"If I were lucky," said the poet, "I might earn a kiss, or if unlucky a dinah."

"A dinah," said the merchant. "By the beard of the Prophet, no bad pay for a mouthful of sweet words. And is it difficult to acquire the trick?"

"All that is needed," answered the poet, "is a rose behind the ear and the moon behind the heart."

"In Damascus," cried the merchant, "I have a hanging garden stained with roses, and at night the moon rises in the garden. My ears are longer than yours, and my heart, if one may judge by a comparison of our persons, is incomparably larger. I will accordingly give up the quest of the goose, and will return to Damascus and in my rose garden lay my own golden eggs. But in the meantime," he added reflectively, stabbing the poet to the heart with the pearl-handled scimitar which he had hitherto concealed, "I may as well dispose of a dangerous rival."

"O fool," whispered the dying poet, "it was only the goose who thought the eggs gold, because of the golden goslings hidden in their cool blue shell, as the peasant discovered when he killed her."

"Why did she think so?" said the merchant, daintily wiping the curved blade.

"Because she was a poet," whispered the dying man. "And why did she tell the peasant?" asked the merchant, preparing to return to his interrupted rest. "Because," said the poet, turning over on his side with a little sigh, "because she was a goose."

"The next story," said the author, "will be an example of grim realism. It will have no characters and no incidents and no meaning. It will continue for some three or four hundred pages, and will begin in the middle and not end at all. There will also be a tendency for verbs and punctuation to disappear simultaneously, and a slightly stagnant atmosphere of muddled gloom will reproduce the sensation of a London fog."

"I did not know," said the publisher, "that you had read Tchekov. For my part I have not, and let me add I do not intend that my public should."

"I do not even know," replied the author, "what Tchekov is, though by the sound it might be a Slavonic parlour game. But if, as always, you are going to thwart me just when I am about to strike a modern note, I will tell you quite simply and (I hope) beautifully an old-fashioned Christmas story. About the year 1840," said the author, "in the City of London, and to be particular in the immediate neighbourhood of a cosy, rosy, prosy old coaching inn in the Borough, lived, or rather existed (for he was a wicked old screw was Jonathan), a merchant in the tea trade (at least he let it be understood that it was the tea trade, but the gossips, who stood about at the street corners with very blue noses waiting for the muffin-boy, had their suspicions that—)"

"I do not," interjected the publisher, "wish to be unduly curious. But may I ask whether there are any other sentences in this story?"

"Of course," retorted the author, with justifiable heat, "but if I am to tell this story at all perhaps you will permit me to tell it in an old-fashioned way. Let me tell you that in 1840 people had time to finish sentences like that, yes and to understand them. A man who could stand the factory system of the time could stand anything."

"Well," continued the author, "there existed in that neighbourhood Jonathan Gogglesnape, and as is general with persons who had acquired names of that sort, he was the hardest, grindingest miser that you would find in a smart day's walk, east, west, south or north of the pump on the left hand corner of the square of St. Runnymede-in-the-East. Jonathan was at all times of the year a cold, pinched figure of a man in a tight, rusty surtout, and not an inch of linen showing either at the mean, scraggy throat or the large red wrists, but at five o'clock on Christmas Eve he was a circumstance, like the whistling wind, to make comfortable folks draw closer to the fire and to thank their Maker and the Spirit of Christmas that they were not as other men.

"A sharp fall of snow, as yet untrodden into filth and mud, had smoothed out the vices of the pavement and given that touch of happy contrast between the radiant revellers within and the homeless wanderers without so typical of Christmas feeling."

"I do not think that I can stand much more of this," said the publisher faintly.

"In that case," said the author, "I shall, without delay, recite a poem which I have called 'In vino veritas.'"

IN VINO VERITAS.

"Singing 'e was. I tell yer, singing as sweet as kiss me 'and—a drunken sort o'chune, but swinging the feet like if yer understand.

"I stood and watched 'is dancin' shadder, Lord wot a dancer! 'eel an' toe. 'Oo's for the ladder—Jacob's ladder—one good 'eave and up yer go!'

"Drunk as God 'e was—the liquor, like a flare of naphthaline, burning as it run, but quicker—brightest thing I ever seen!

"'Appy? well I arsk yer! Drinking, laughing, singing, dance 'e went, Tell yer straight I kep' on thinking—'appy! that's wot 'appy meant.

"'I've a ladder—Jacob's ladder—one good 'eave and up yer go. Men are mad, but God is madder—' Meaning? 'Ow am I ter know?'

"Laughing, singing, dancing, mumming—looking soft and sly behind 'im, 'Are yer coming? Aren't yer coming?' Damn 'is eyes—I'm off to find 'im."

"There is a good deal," remarked the publisher, "to be said for Prohibition."

XXV

TANTAE RELIGIO

And another thing. In the gardens of Haroun-al-Raschid, just past the corner where one pale rose watches her tranquil shadow in the ice-blue water of a marbled pond, grew a black tree that could not wait for the Arabian spring. But on the contrary, instead of leaves she threw over her graceful shoulders a cloak sprigged with red blossom. And that in a single night.

"Oh miracle," said the first gardener next morning when he observed this bright irregularity, "red snow has fallen in the night." "Oh marvel," said the second, "a swarm of red butterflies." "Oh wonder," cried the third, "a little lanthorn in each lighted twig." "You must be blind," said the first; "or a numbskull," said the second; "or mad," cried the third. And thereupon, as was only to be expected, the three fell to fighting furiously one with another.

"What are those men doing?" whispered the terrified blossoms to the mother tree; "we are afraid."

"Hush! blossoms," murmured the tree, "they think that we are a divine manifestation."

"What is that?" asked the blossoms.

"The appearance of the God they worship upon earth," replied the tree.

"And how do you know," cried the blossoms, "that they think so?"

"Because," said the tree as the last gardener fell heavily to the ground, "they are killing one another."

XXVI

ON ENTERTAINING ANGELS UNAWARES

The pale-faced man with the slightly Jewish cast of countenance was observed for the first time on the night of the 27th June passing through the churchyard by the Vicar, who, taking him, not unnaturally, for a loafer, ordered him out pretty sharply. He obeyed with remarkable meekness and disappeared rapidly in the direction of the house of Mrs. Bolpus. He was next seen on the following evening—a cold, clear night of moon—by the village ninny, or so it was supposed. For he came back shouting some nonsense about a lighted man, and laughed happily and quietly all night.

It was, however, her ladyship who met him in broad daylight two days later, and engaged him in conversation. For she had heard of his appearance and feared that he might be a new scandal. She had intended to begin by speaking to him roundly, but something soft and flickering in his eyes stopped her. Instead of reproving him, therefore, she said, speaking almost as to an equal:

"We are thinking of forming a branch of the Society of Poor Lost Things in the village, and we wondered whether you would care to join?" "Strange," he replied in a low but beautifully clear voice, "I was also thinking of forming a society. But perhaps our objects are the same! What is yours?" "Oh," said the lady, "we aim at sweetening bitter lives."

"In that case," said the stranger earnestly, "I would like to give all I have. It is, I fear," he added with a smile, "only a guinea."

"You are joking, I see," murmured the lady, signing a receipt with a gold pencil. "And now, sir, will you forgive me if I make a personal observation?"

"But of course," he replied.

"You are lodging with Mrs. Bolpus. As a stranger you cannot know her reputation. If I might without impertinence suggest it, perhaps it would be wise to find a less questionable landlady."

"And yet," mused the stranger, "she seemed poor and unhappy."

"And so she should," cut in the lady.

"Indeed I should have described her as a Poor Lost Thing."

"I can see," said the benefactress icily, taking the guinea out of her purse, "that you have misunderstood the objects of the Society. We assist only the deserving." "In my Society," said the man, sadly pocketing his coins, "we assist first the undeserving."

"So I should imagine," sneered her ladyship, "and what do you call it?"

"Oh," said the stranger gently, turning away, "we call it the Society of the Rich Lost Things, for whom the way to the kingdom of heaven is through the eye of a needle."

"I hope," said her ladyship to the Earl, her husband, at dinner, "that you will arrange for Mrs. Bolpus to be evicted at once."

"Evicted!" said the Earl; "but haven't you heard the news? She died this morning."

"Died!" gasped the lady; "then what was the Jew with the beard doing in her house?"

"The Jew with the beard?" asked her husband. "I was there to-day and didn't hear of anyone."

"Are you sure?" cried the Countess.

"Quite!" said the Earl, "but wait! Is it perhaps the tramp that the Vicar saw in the churchyard and poor Geordie Brown's 'lighted man'? I think myself that in both cases it was just imagination."

"Perhaps," replied the lady after a long pause, "but all the same I shall resign my chairmanship of the branch of the Poor Lost Things."

"Now what in the name of God—," began the Earl.

"Hush," almost screamed his wife.

XXVII

TEMPUS FUGIT

"No," said the old grandfather clock to the green parrot, "I will not tell you another story. I have told so many that I am quite hoarse." "I cannot think what you mean," replied the parrot. "You have said nothing but tick-tock like a hen, and then you cluck loudly as though you had laid an egg, though you have in fact only mislaid an hour. That is not my idea of a story."

"When you are my age," said the clock, "you will realise that there is no other story."

XXVIII

YOU CAN TAKE A HORSE TO THE WATER

Once upon a time (and you will see later that it was fortunately not twice upon this time) in the garden of the Château of Nyon, in the sweet heart of a lime tree and very near to the little padded box where they keep the silkworms, there lived a chrysalis, whose ancestors had come over with John Knox, but who nevertheless agreed with Hume.

"The Almighty," he said, speaking with what he conceived to be a Scottish accent, "is merely a prrojection of the chrysalis mind—a varra puir exemple of the association of incomparable ideas. Now Kant, as every Scotsman knows, dragged in the soul—a silly bit fluttering thing with white wings—the great gowk. Mon, it's a peety...."

"Qu'est que tu me chantes là," exclaimed an elderly silk-worm, who was busily occupied in his exquisite occupation. "Execrable worm, thinkest thou that because thou art no better than a dried twig that all suffer from such misfortune? It is indeed certain that upon such as thee the good God has not wasted a soul, but as to me I know that the delicate machine which can spin so marvellous a net was not meant to fade into dust. But what can one expect of one whose forefathers were generated in a fog, lived in an east wind, and died without ever having seen the sun?" and with this the silk-worm resumed his tapestry.

"What," exclaimed the chrysalis, "is it Scotland you're naming in the same breath wi' your God-forgotten, pope-ridden, frog-warren? A'm black ashamed, ah am, and metaphysic or no a'll no ha it said that any trapesing piece of a Frenchy had a soul and me from the Clachans of the Tolbooth no. But mind," he added as he burst, and from his husk daintily, like a lace handkerchief out of lavender, rose the butterfly, "my opeenions remain unchanged."

"I also," said the silk-worm, "who have all the years had faith, will take wings." And he breathed very hard and deep, but the only result was that he spoiled his skein.

XXIX

HALF A LOAF IS BETTER THAN NO BREAD

Once upon a time there lived in a cathedral city, almost in the shadow of the minster, a middle-aged freethinker, who was exceedingly angry with God for not existing. Nor was he conciliated by those who pointed out (reasonably enough) that it was not His fault. This, in the view of the freethinker, merely increased the offence. "He should have thought of all that before," he would say grimly.

In the same town, but actually in the minster itself, yes and in a hole in the pulpit, lived a mouse, who, for her part, did not agree with the freethinker. She was, I fear, not as independent a mind as she should have been, and permitted herself to be influenced by the singularly sweet voice of the principal officiating priest. Him she (foolishly) identified with the creator of the ample mansion of her choice, and indeed let it be understood among her acquaintance that she was peculiarly acceptable in his sight. "For," she said, "every day he comes dressed all in white when the sun strikes through the windows, throwing a coloured shadow on his robe, and scatters precious bread for me on a stainless cloth. And in further proof," she would say to scoffers, "there is a second and lesser angel, who salutes him, calling him by his name of 'Our Father in Heaven.'" Several mice who doubted her story came at her invitation to scoff and remained to eat the sacred crumbs.

Now it was exactly this matter of the bread which above all other Christian uses most inflamed the freethinker. When he was not railing at the superstition of those who believed that a celestial body could be concealed in milled and baked ears of corn, he was complaining against the waste of good bread. He would calculate a statistic of the annual diversion of bread to this purpose. "Think of the poor!" he would snort, but it is not certain that he thought of them himself.

The freethinker's habit in the spring months of the year was to take an early turn along the quiet and flowery streets. The clean and morning beauty was for him an anodyne, and when he was certain of escaping observation he would on occasion slip through a small postern gate in the cathedral and brood happily upon the base uses to which a structure so noble had been addressed. During one of these intrusions he observed that the cloth was laid on the high altar and that the priest was preparing the communion service. As no worshippers appeared, the freethinker drew near to the altar in order to satisfy himself by personal witness of the futility of the celebration.

The priest did not observe (or did not appear to observe) his visitor, but completed the ritual as though in the company of a great host. "Buffoonery!" muttered the freethinker, struggling angrily against the radiant charm of the sun falling through old glass. "Bad enough," he continued in an audible whisper, "to serve bread to those who do not need it, but to serve it to nobody at all—!!"

"Are you sure," said the priest, who had finished the service, "that it is for nobody?" and he pointed smiling to the tiny grey communicants nibbling the crumbs. "Do I understand," inquired the freethinker icily, "that you perform this service for the sake of the mice?" "Why not," said the priest; "as you do to the least of these—" "This," said the freethinker, quite properly indignant, "is what I should call blasphemy." "And of that," said the priest, turning to go to the vestry, "you should be no mean judge."

"Sir," said the verger to the priest later in the day, "them mice have been about again. I see two of them at the sacred bread. I wish you would let me set traps." "Why," said the priest, "I have already set one." "And did you catch anything?" asked the verger. "I think so," said the priest.

XXX

IN FOR A PENNY IN FOR A POUND

There was once a beautiful line of poetry who had by an unfortunate accident lodged herself in the brain of an extremely inferior poet. To her great discomfort the line found herself driven to associate with a disorderly mob of worn-out and shabby phrases. Nor was this all. While her companions were for ever being taken out and aired, and on occasion finding their way into the public prints, she remained neglected and disused.

The other lines, who had from the first disliked her, now, not unnaturally, added contempt to their dislike. "The truth is," they said to her, "that you are not one of us. The rest of us can all point to a long and distinguished ancestry. Everybody knew our parents and knows us. We are welcome wherever we go, and are readily admitted into the best society. But as for you, your birth is wrapt in mystery. Whether it is the fact that the poet is your father is open to question, but at any rate there is no question whatever of the character of the Greek woman your mother. You had better," they would conclude, "return whence you came, where, among persons of your own kind, you will no doubt be at ease."

The poet, meanwhile, only dimly aware of his golden visitor, continued to fumble among his ready-for-service shelves. This was the easier for him as all his ideas were of stock size, and were in consequence easily fitted by the poetic slops. But as time went on the poet became more and more acutely aware of something that waited expression—some queer new-shaped Jack o' lanthorn of a thought that none of his ready-made suits would fit. One after another he took them down, and they seemed incorrigibly stale and shop-soiled. Even the most daring patterns in the earlier Brooke design seemed inadequate, out at the seams and unfresh.

He blamed his liver. Then he blamed his wife, and last—most horrible thought of all—he blamed his inspiration. "I have written myself out," he cried to the pool of light that the lamp cast on his solitary desk. "This is the end." He rehearsed in a high tragic voice some of his most notable triumphs, as for example:

"Now that the roses are over
And the last white rose is dead, Quiet returns to the lover
Instead....

"Instead of love freely given
To love that asked for no price, Instead of a boy in Heaven
And a girl in Paradise,

"Now that the roses are over
And the last white rose is dead, Quiet returns to the lover
Instead.

"My God!" he cried to the unreceptive almond blossoms on the wall-paper. "What genius I had when I wrote that."

He sat down at the desk and looked severely at the virgin page. No neat rhymes again, no passion tied up in brown paper and looped with string for a finger, no beauty sent home with the first delivery. "This," he repeated with melancholy grandeur, "is the end."

And at that directly minute he saw a line form itself in letters of flame along the page, as though a candle wrote it—a lovely line with the sovereign note of Cleopatra's cry:

"O infinite virtue, comest thou smiling from   the world's great snare uncaught?"

For one wild moment his spirit, overlaid with swathe upon swathe of rubbish, moved upwards to the light. For whatever he was now, he had once been a poet, if only in his hopes. In that luminous instant he almost guessed his failure. "The end," he muttered; "suppose it were the beginning?" With that the old lines that had suffered defeat resumed their empire. "Yes, the beginning," he cried, "the beginning," and radiant he began to write, sure of his inspiration:

"It's the call of love: 'Oh follow where my golden footsteps tread!' But the call of love is hollow by the calling of the dead."

So, with head bent, he continued writing through the night. And while he wrote the other lines turned upon the bastard and drove her into the dark.

"What a beautiful poem," said the editor of his favourite journal when it was sent to him. "Not so bad," said the poet modestly. "The fact is, it all started with a line—a direct inspiration." "What was it?" inquired the editor languidly. "Well, to be perfectly honest," replied the poet, "I've forgotten it."

XXXI

QUANTITY IS BETTER THAN QUALITY

"This is the thirty-first story," said the publisher; "how many more do you propose to write?" "The question you should have asked," replied the author, "is how many less?" "Less than what?" inquired the publisher irritably. "Less than what I could if I'm not stopped. I am like the princess who when she opened her mouth breathed jewels, which her detractors alleged were toads—jewels, I would observe, four words long which on the stretched forefinger—" "I have my own opinion," said the publisher firmly, "on the question of jewels and toads! I think forty would constitute a full drove or clutch, or whatever a group of that species is called." "Very well," said the author, deeply affronted, "I will now tell you the sad incident which I am bound, in view of your attack upon me, to call 'Quantity is better than Quality.'

"There was once," said the author, "in the eastern marches of a highly-constitutionalised monarchy, a society whose members were pledged to breathe only once a week. They aspired by the force of this remarkable example to discourage the distressing continuity of breathing among the lower classes. Now it must be obvious at once that even well-born persons could only impose this limitation upon themselves if assisted by nature. And nature had assisted them. For to reveal the truth (which they had concealed from the warm-blooded proletariat), they were not only blue-blooded but actually cold-blooded. It will be seen therefore that their action, though in itself meritorious, involved a less sacrifice than was commonly represented by their champions.

"From the outset their efforts were openly derided by the lowest classes, who, so far from ceasing to breathe, if anything breathed more and louder than ever. But fortunately in that country there was a middling class—known for purposes of reference as the backbone of the country—who knew how to value their social superiors. These, therefore, with much agony and spiritual exercise, began to practise the new mode, letting it be gradually understood that breathing was vulgar. Their contortions, as may well be imagined, afforded much amusement to the society and received, as was right, a considerable measure of public approbation at their hands. Unluckily, however, the middling class tended to carry the matter too far. For in their excess of zeal they not only reduced the amount of their breathing, but even ceased breathing altogether. In such cases the formula 'He (or she) is not dead but sleeps' was generally applied. For no one would admit the social disgrace of being dead.

"Nobody knows how long this engaging state of affairs would have continued if it had not been for a cessation of work by the Banded Guild of Sextons and Gravediggers. These simple fellows naturally welcomed the increase of business that came their way as the result of the new fashion. But unhappily they became involved in a serious demarcation dispute with another association—"The Society of Critics, Essayists and Writers of Belles Lettres." This latter body, it had always been recognised, were alone entitled to bury the living (with a subsidiary function of resurrecting the dead). They protested accordingly with the greatest vigour against the invasion of their sphere by a guild whose affair was solely (as their own rules showed) with the dead.

"The Government of the country, quite properly and according to the accepted practice, attempted to hush the matter up. But the Society of Critics were able by virtue of their association with the newspaper press to defeat this laudable endeavour. To the disgust of the remainder of the middling class, and in spite of the advice freely tendered by some of the older soldiers among the upper class, to the effect that the matter should be decided by the general execution of all members of both rival bodies, the question was remitted for decision to an impartial arbitrator. After a long hearing and the most anxious consideration this gentleman issued his award. It was a long and cogently written document, and aroused general dissatisfaction. For among other illuminating observations, he pointed out that if a man is only as old as he feels, then, a fortiori, he is only as dead as he admits. This was generally regarded by the critics as a decision in their favour. On the other hand, the sextons drew attention to another portion of the report, in which the arbitrator eloquently reminded those who had appointed him that his countrymen, whose proud boast was that they did not know when they were beaten, would still less be likely to know when they were dead. His final recommendation was, however, equally distasteful to both parties. For he concluded by observing that to those who were of like mind with him there was no death. He would refer to M. Maeterlinck, the well-known Belgian expert on bees: 'Death,' he began in a passage long after quoted in the schools, 'is the door of life.'

"The issue being thus left in doubt, the sextons—warm-blooded as they were and breathing noisily—cut the knot by a general cessation of work. The critics, though invited by an enthusiastic press to show their quality, restricted themselves to stating publicly that the pen was mightier than the spade, and leaving it there.

"The deadlock was only resolved by announcement on the part of the head of the Government (the coldness of whose blood was sufficiently established to condone any eccentricity) that in future he for one would breathe continuously. To which an even colder (and bluer) blooded colleague of ducal rank added that he would not merely breathe but actually snore.

"It was, however, made clear that this announcement was entirely spontaneous and had no connection with the deplorable stoppage of work. In the result the middling class resumed their breathing. The sextons returned to their diminished labours, and the critics, discovering a new and living novelist of genius, set about his interment with renewed vigour. And thus," concluded the author, "we see that Quantity is better than Quality."

"Talking of toads," said the publisher. "Yes," replied the author, "let us talk of them. I remember that they have jewels in their foreheads." "Then yours," snarled the publisher, "must have turned their backs."

XXXII

CHARITY BEGINS AT HOME

From time to time, or rather from eternity to eternity, Ormuzd finds himself inconvenienced by the perpetual praise offered up to him by the blesséd. Though he is very anxious not to hurt their feelings, he cannot but wonder whether such complete absence of the critical faculty constitutes the best of company.

It is in this mood that Ahriman, always sensitive to the All-Highest emotions, ventures to appear and exchange insults with the Senior Power. And he has a double reason. He has a perfectly devilish capacity for feeling sorry for himself in exile. It is, however, more than that. Like Ormuzd, he is concerned not to wound the susceptibilities of his constituents, but some eternities he permits himself to ask whether uninterrupted blasphemies may not jar an ear specially designed for their reception.

"This constant preoccupation with another place," he would think, "is not very flattering to me."

"And so, my poor Ahriman," Ormuzd would say on these occasions, "you are still dissatisfied? But I do not see what more I can do for you. I have given you rule over half the universe. I cannot give you the power to enjoy it."

"No, sire," replies the impudent fiend, "since charity begins at home—if I may describe heaven by so inappropriate a title."

"Shall I tell you," says Ormuzd, "what really ails you, Ahriman? It is not that evil is a mocker, not that it tears down idols, and least of all that it is outrageously clever. The painful truth, on the contrary," says Ormuzd gently, "is that evil is so stupid." This, as may be supposed, wounds Ahriman in a very tender spot.

"Sire," says he, "if it were possible for you to be unjust I should so describe that observation. For consider! All round with the docility of inspired sheep the blameless lift their monotonous outcries. They worship what is worshipful, I allow, but how without perception of its subtleties, of its trembling poise upon the edge of disaster. The blessed croon like old women before the fire, but they do not guess (or care) that the roots of the flame are in hell."

"But you are still stupid," answers Ormuzd, "for these adore what they do not understand, while you hate what you insist on misunderstanding. Here am I, Ormuzd—a symbol, a golden knob on a door that none can press—a veil of silver—and here are you, Ahriman, also an ebon metaphor of what is too dark to be apprehended. And yet, poor Ahriman, you being so dark a ghost rail upon me being a ghost so bright. But what of that which is behind us both?"

"Ormuzd," says Ahriman, "you cannot cheat me thus. You are a thing in my mind, as I am a thing in yours, and if our thoughts cease, both of us cease with them. After us the Deluge."

"It is true," says Ormuzd, "that the thing you see is made up of your sight, but it is not true of me. For that is the difference between good and evil. I know that I am nothing, but you believe (falsely) that you are everything."

"Humility," sneers the fiend, "sits ill on the thundering lips of Ormuzd."

"Truth," replies Ormuzd, "is neither proud nor humble; it is."

"What is truth?" mocks the fiend, preparing to go. "I suppose that you will tell me that you are the truth."

"No," says Ormuzd, "it is because you deny that I am truth and secretly believe it that you are Ahriman, but it is because I know that I am not the truth that I am Ormuzd."

"I have enjoyed our little chat," says Ahriman, "but you lack ambition."

"By that sin—" begins Ormuzd.

"Oh, nonsense," cries Ahriman hotly, and then repents of his rudeness. "Forgive me, sire, but I could believe in you if you believed in yourself."

"Ahriman, Ahriman," says Ormuzd, laughing lightly, "still tempting me!"

"I bear you no grudge," says Ahriman. "The truth is—"

"Yes?" asks Ormuzd.

"That you are too clever for me."

"I thought we should come to it in the end," says Ormuzd.

XXXIII

DIS ALITER VISUM

At the beginning of the nineteenth century, somewhere in Germany there was a neat little town with gabled houses and a platform for the stork in the market-place. There was nothing remarkable about this town or its people. By day the houses slumbered cosily and the men went about their cobbling, saddling, and carpentry with the best will in the world. At evening lights were shown at the windows, and within doors the husbands smoked their long pipes with their pot of beer close at hand, and the wives sewed innumerable patches on innumerable small pants. In spring and summer tables were set in the trim garden, and at evening a stranger passing down the cobbled street would have seen amiable family groups each under their linden-tree absorbing their evening meal. And sometimes one more given to sentiment than another might divide the calm evening air with some monotonous ditty locally assumed to be music. But the great day was Sunday. Then the whole township, with bent heads, moved to the church, where the pastor preached the virtues of the ideal, of charity, and of peace. And his flock, as harmless as any other sheep, from time to time bleated sympathetically and with the air of impending sleep. And later in the day the same pastor, who was something of a poet, would often collect a group round him in the schoolroom and tell them one of the "Märchen," to which even the grown-ups were never tired of listening.

As you may suppose, among other stories he would often tell them the tale of "Schneevitchen," or, as we call it, "Snow-white." The jealous stepmother, the mirror of beauty, the poisoned apple, the dwarfs and the sleeping lovely were murmured into the inner conscience of his audience. And so all might have continued till the end of time. The little town might have dusked and shone night and day, the quiet inhabitants have gone about their business, lived and died, and new storks replaced the old ones on the platform. All this, I say, might have happened if two strangers had not come to the little town and settled in a vacant house almost next door to that of the pastor. They were, so it was understood, husband and wife, though many wondered how two persons so repulsive could ever have endured that relationship. The man was not otherwise ill-looking, but so thin that in certain lights you would have sworn that you could see his very bones, and there were those who declared that the wind would have whistled through him if it had not been for his absurdly ill-fitting clothes. The woman, on the other hand, was fat, not with a comfortable tissue, but with a gross hardness that forbade all friendliness. She was not a monstrosity, save at meals, when she ate like a beast out of the woods, hugely, violently, and with the worst manners in the world.

At the outset they were regarded with suspicion. For though they were good customers of the shops and paid cash, no one could deny that they were ugly customers. There was, further, something queer about their name. It was not a decent German one with a flavour of wurst about it, but was a queer foreign one. For it was plain that the baker, who had written it down as Tod, must have misheard the gentleman, while the grocer must have equally misunderstood the lady when he entered her upon his books as Krieg. Moreover, though the man let it be understood that he was widely known as a preacher, they did not at first attend service with the rest of the community.

It is probable that their influence would never have attained any hold if the old pastor had lived. For first and last, though he was the gentlest of men, he would none of them. But as is the way with the gentlest as with those most rude, he fell upon a heavy sickness. The physician of the town was in despair, and finally, hearing that the stranger had a great reputation as a healer, invited him into consultation. In this way, for the first time, Herr Todt (if that were his name) crossed the old pastor's threshold.

"We meet at last," said the stranger. "Aye," said the dying man, looking him fearlessly in the sunken eyes, "but you have no sting for me." "I fear," said the stranger, turning to the local physician, "that he is delirious; I can do nothing." "You have done all you can," cried the good old man, "and you have failed. But oh, my flock, my flock!" "They are in safe hands," said the stranger mildly. "See, rest yours in them and feel how easy they are." With a wild gesture the pastor swept them away. "Retro me, Sathanas," he cried madly; "not into your hands," but, with a deep peace stealing over him, "in tuas manus, Domine."

The whole town attended the burial, and in the absence of any other priest the stranger, who, it was understood, had taken holy orders, committed the body to the earth. There was a profound grief for the loss of one so simple, so friendly, so full of harmless kindness and dreams. But more than that, many of the older men felt that a period had ended with their pastor's death. "There," said one returning homewards, "lies old Germany."

After this Herr Dr. Todt and his wife moved into the presbytery, and in some way never fully explained he became the officiating priest. It became noticeable almost at once that while the older men found him increasingly distasteful, all the younger men and most of the older women fell entirely under his sway. Nor was this surprising, for he preached a new and striking doctrine. In his first sermon he took for his text, "I come to bring, not peace, but a sword," and for the first time in the quiet cobbled streets there was a faint far-off echo of trampling steel. He went from strength to strength, till for those who followed him he seemed almost more than human—almost a new Saint John, but one who, in preparing the way for his Lord, made it rough for all feet save His. But yet among the older men there were those that murmured unquietly of blasphemy and those who said openly that he declared himself the way of salvation, and even called him the Antichrist. But Dr. Todt cared for none of these things.

Nor was this all, for his wife began to exercise an influence equal to, if not greater than, her husband's. (She had, by the way, cleared away the muddle as to names by explaining that she was a geborene Krieg, and had assumed her husband's name on marriage.) Frau Dr. Todt continued the Sunday evening meetings in the schoolroom, but they were no longer a place where old men turned from the fireside to listen to the memories of childhood. Far from it. The talk she held was of glory, of the old wars, and of a helmetted god called Wotan. And it was observed that in a strange indefinable way for those who attended her meetings she lost her ugliness. They swore that she was not old, nor fat, nor a guzzler, but young and slender and endowed with the swift feet of the Valkyries. So fair did the young men find her that they began even to forget their loves. But when their sweethearts complained the young men put them aside, saying that she was not a rival but their mother. "Your mother!" cried the young women, "are you mad?" "It is only a way of speaking," said the young men. "She is the voice of Germany. Have you not heard the new gospel?" and one among them repeated the strange, harsh lines:

"You have conquered, Arminius! The Roman world has grown red with your breath, and its beauty is perished and no man wonders or weeps at its death!

"Again as the meshes drew near us you heard the buccina crack on the last high whisper, 'O Varrus, give me my legions back!'

"You had twisted your web together in triumph, but Wotan was dumb, for he watched a gold eagle's feather, and he saw the lost legions come.

"Since scarce had the Northern Valkyries been whistled by Wotan home ere the eagles flew back to their eyries, on the hills of a greater Rome.

"And Wotan to Arminius leaning, whispered, 'Though conquest is sweet you have lost your own soul in the winning, now capture the world's in defeat.'

"You have conquered but only the bodies, and the spirit is more than the flesh; now weave for the soul and where God is deep in the heart the mesh."

"You are all mad together," cried the girls. "This means nothing. What is Wotan to us or we to him?" "This is the new world which we are making," said the young men, and returned to the feet of their teacher.

But there was one girl in the town who would not give up the fight so easily. She was the daughter of the old pastor, and for her fairness and gentleness and soft beauty had been called "Schneevitchen." Like her father before her, she had steady grey eyes, and like him she knew the old songs of Germany that (some said) were echoes of the song of the Niebelung—gold girls in the river Rhine. She alone could hold her head against the now predominant pair, and she became in consequence the object of their deadly hate. For often, when the young men crowded round her, Frau Todt geborene Krieg would look into the young men's eyes as into a mirror and say:

"Mirror, mirror on the wall, am I fairest of them all?"

And she would see in their eyes the shadow of "Schneevitchen." She and her husband consulted together, and finally they compounded an apple of sweet essences, which she pretended had grown on a tree in the Hesperides, but to her husband she confessed that it was no such thing and that its real name was Discord. This she gave not to Snow-white to eat, but to the young men, and straightway they were poisoned. For they began to have ugly dreams and see swart visions, and always in the dark heart of them was Snow-white, no longer pure, gentle and loving, but the Lorelei drawing into her whirlpool drowning men.

There are many tales of how she came to perish in the broad river. Some say she drowned herself, some say the young men, bewildered, cast her into the waters, and others that the strangers flung her into the great body of the stream. None knows. But what is known is that with her death in that little town and in many other towns great and small the old pastor and his daughter were forgotten, and in their place ruled over hearts and minds Herr Doktor Todt and his wife, the geborene Krieg.

XXXIV

PARALLEL LINES DO NOT MEET

This is quite a different sort of story. It is about a princess who disbelieved in arithmetic.

"Was she a French princess?" inquired the publisher.

"Certainly not," said the author, "and I cannot think why you should suppose that she was. On the contrary, she lived in Hammersmith Broadway, and took the view that there was no reason why parallel lines should not meet. 'Why,' she would ask, 'should they be snobs just because they happen to be parallel? Besides,' she would add, 'when I draw them they do meet.'"

"But," said a celebrated professor from the London School of Economics who had been summoned by her anxious parents to cope with the situation, "those lines which you have drawn aren't parallel."

"Why?" inquired the princess.

"Why?" said the professor, "but it is obvious to anybody. Can't you see that they meet?"

"Yes," said the princess, "I see that, but that is what I call being parallel."

"But can't you see that you are defying the axioms upon which all cognition is based. If parallel lines meet, then when I meet you you do not meet me."

"I see no harm in that," said the princess, who, to be perfectly honest, had formed a (quite unjustly) low opinion of the professor's social gifts; "but speaking of axioms, would you agree that God is omnipotent?"

"Certainly," said the professor, "but I do not see how—"

"Forgive me," said the princess icily. "If God is omnipotent should he not be able to draw parallel lines that meet?"

"You will forgive my observing," said the professor, "that if God interfered with mathematics he would cease to be God."

"And if mathematics interfered with God?" inquired the princess.

"I cannot," said the professor, slapping his tall hat on his head with a resounding bang, "waste my time in talking nonsense."

"You could, however," cried the princess after him, "give up teaching mathematics, could you not?"

XXXV

CHERCHEZ LE JUIF

"I will now," said the author, "without more ado tell the true story of Rumpelstiltskin. It was, I think, Professor Boxer, of a celebrated university, who traced in it a complete articulation of the Hittite sun-mythology. He was not deceived by the superficial appearance of elegant nonsense. He observed that Rumpel (as he called him for short), like Jahwe, laid great stress on concealing his true name. Nor did he believe that it was likely that even Rumpel was anything other than a disguise. 'Who?' he effectively inquired, 'would answer to such a name?' Clearly, he concluded the name was one of which the utterance might be supposed to unloose the struts of the world. Now, for my part, I cannot go the whole way with Professor Boxer. That the story has a deep symbolism nobody, least of all one who makes his livelihood by the pretence, would deny. But that it is Hittite in origin, no one who has studied the customs of that astounding people the Hivites would for a moment assert. Taking first the evidence of the Rosetta stone, what do we find?"

"That you have lately been on a personally conducted tour round the British Museum," harshly interrupted the publisher.

"And if I have," cried the author, "am I to be forbidden the simple pleasure of showing off to my readers who have not had a similar experience? Am I to have no humanity, no expansion, no freedom? In short, am I writing this book, or are you?"

"If you are going to take that line," said the publisher, "you will force me to inquire on whom the financial risk falls? With income-tax—"

"Very well," said the author. "As I detest bickering, I will handle the story differently, though I am not prepared to abandon my Hivites."

"That damned old Jew," began the representative of the well-known Hittite newspaper....

"Hush," said his Hivite colleague in the press gallery of the Convention of the Association of Peoples, "here he is."

"It is my belief," muttered the Hittite, "that he is the authentic Wandering Jew. He appears with his white beard and his parcel at all international meetings. I believe he is a plague-carrier! Good-day," he added aloud, "Monsieur Moses that goes always well!"

The white-bearded old man deposited his heavy parcel with a sigh. "As usual," he said, "I find nobody to relieve me of this." "It would seem very heavy," said the Hivite. "It is very heavy," said the old Jew; "try to lift it." The Hivite bent down and strained with all his strength. The parcel shifted not an inch.

"Heavens!" he said, looking respectfully at the old man. "You must be strong. But what is it—lead or gold?"

"The name you call the metal," said the old man wearily, "is a matter of taste. It is at any rate difficult to support, in which, as your Hittite colleague is thinking, it is not unlike me." "My God! what a suggestion," said the Hittite, whose true thought had been accurately expressed. "But, putting on one side your play of spirit, tell us as among colleagues what is your object?" "To hand over my charge to one worthy to carry it," said the old man. "And do you expect to find him among this collection of international lawmongers?" inquired the Hittite. "Where else?" said the Jew. "Do you, then," inquired the Hivite, "believe in international law?" "I sometimes pretend," said the old man, smilingly, "that I invented it. But pardon me! The ceremony is about to begin."

The hall below was filled to overflowing. All the delegations were in their places, all showing in their dress that the occasion was one of a very especial character. From the press gallery, which was behind the platform on which the president and the officers of the Convention sat, could be observed the veiled statue of International Concord, which the president was that day to dedicate. Almost immediately that gentleman, followed by a train, beribboned like himself, walked solemnly on to the platform and took his seat.

The delegations settled down to listen to his speech, anticipating, as they were entitled to upon his reputation, a superb effort. But before the president could rise to speak a delegate from East Oceania rose to a point of order. He was anxious to do nothing to mar the harmony of so auspicious an occasion, but he wished to know whether any arrangements had been made as to the order of speeches. He represented a small country, but one no less passionately devoted to the cause of international concord than some of those larger ones, owing to whose ambition his country found itself so reduced.

The president rose to observe that any delegate who desired would, if he caught his eye, be heard. On such an occasion it would be suitable that representatives of all classes of nations should be heard. The representative of West Oceania rose to inquire what was meant by classes of nations. Was this an indirect gibe at the smaller nations? If so, he would observe that they had suffered enough already at the hands of their great neighbours. The president, who had risen to express the hope that delegates would not indulge in controversy, was interrupted by the delegate from Central Oceania, who observed that on behalf of his Government he indignantly repudiated the calumnies that had fallen from the lips of the last two speakers. It was owing to the strong hand of nations such as his that this glorious scene of international amity was achieved. And to drive home that assertion, let him remind the Convention that the symbol of concord chosen, namely a griffin, was the emblem of his State.

The president again endeavoured to closure the discussion, but was forced to give way to the delegate of the Eurasian Empire, who said that while he entirely agreed with the general position taken up by his Central Oceanic colleague, he was bound to correct him on a point of detail. The design which had been approved by the Commission, of which he had had the honour of acting as chairman, was not a griffin, but the bull of Melem-to-Pek, his country's ensign. The Trans-Oceanic delegate demanded the word. Upon its being granted, he remarked that not for the first time had the Eurasian Empire endeavoured to confuse the issue. As the result of what he was bound to call an unfortunate alliance with the Hivites—contrary to the spirit of the international tables—that empire believed that with its ally it could dictate to the whole world. Fortunately, however, those who, like his country and their friends, the Hittites, believed in internationalism were not prepared to stand by and see this robber combination—The Hivite and Eurasian delegates leapt to their feet amid a growing volume of cries. When order was restored it was observed that the delegate of Prester John had the floor. He desired simply to observe that the symbol, for what it was worth, was merely a dragon, the sign of the oldest culture in the world. When the barbarians of the West

The tumult was renewed, and this time the president found himself quite unable to cope with the situation. At last a member of the secretariat in the gallery had the brilliant idea of tugging at the cord which suspended the veil. As it fell a sudden hush fell on the crowd, and then as the gold image was revealed the cries were renewed: "The Griffin of Central Oceania," "The Bull of Melem-to-Pek," "The Gold Dragon," "The Hesperidan Sheep."

"Silence!" roared a voice of thunder.

All the delegates paused in utter astonishment and looked at the press gallery, whence this outrageous interjection had proceeded. There they observed the old Jew standing transfigured and terrible.

"Fools," he said, "do you not see that it is a golden calf?" and with that, before anyone could speak or interfere, he drew a shining object from his parcel and aimed it at the image, shattering it to fragments.

In a moment the whole Convention were on their feet, shouting and cursing. A rush was made for the gallery, but the old Jew was not to be found. When those on the platform examined the missile it was discovered to be a great stone tablet inscribed with Hebrew characters. Unfortunately there was nobody present who knew that language. Some, however, said that it was a rival code of honour known among the Jews as "The Ten Points" or "The Ten Commandments," but others (and these were the large majority) saw in it only a further proof of the well-known Jewish determination to destroy civilisation.

On the motion of the Philistine delegation, it was unanimously decided to exclude the Jews from the Association of Peoples. International harmony having thus been restored, the president was enabled to deliver his speech, which, it was generally agreed, was a magnificent contribution to the cause of international peace and goodwill.

XXXVI

[Greek: GNÔTHI SEAUTON]

They had shown the newcomer all the sights of the place—Peter's great keys, the alabaster walls, the sword of Michael, and Gabriel's last trumpet. At last they brought him to the greatest wonder of all—the glass, in which all his life he had seen darkly. "Look," they said, "for now you shall see God face to face." He looked at first with unspeakable awe, then with surprise, last with bitter disappointment. "I am not judged worthy," he said, turning sorrowfully away, "I saw nothing but myself."

XXXVII

E PUR SI MUOVE

It is not easy to exaggerate the emotion excited in the better elements in the simian world when Bandar, the umbrella-faced ape, announced his theory that apes were evolved from men. It was not merely the blasphemous suggestion that the great Baboon had not, as inspired writing showed, made apes in his own image. That was bad enough, though it tended to upset the more serious-minded rather than the general. But what outraged the public taste and wounded it in its tenderest point was the impudent and indeed grossly indelicate contention that there had been a time when monkeys had no tails. What made it worse, however, was the damnable plausibility of it all. Even the most prejudiced could hardly fail to recognise with a shudder of disgust faint far-off simian traits, loathsomely humanised, but still distinguishable in men. To take physique first. It was perhaps true that the mean, chinless face was entirely wanting in the higher bestiality. Yet it could not be denied that men had been observed (notably during the recent disturbances, when they had so continually killed one another) with a promise of the true prognathous chin. Then as to the withered little arms and the long deformed lower limbs, with their flattened pads, it could not be disputed that in their cities the men grew more ape-like in both respects, with arms increasingly long and grasping and legs proportionally short and unmanlike. It was true that no instance had ever been known of a man with a tail. But on the other hand, Bandar pointed out that among certain degenerate types of the larger ape, as for example the Mandril, tails were far less developed than among the better sort. Then as to habits and manners. Here the likeness was even more disconcerting. First, in the matter of food, it was true that for the most part they had the horrible human habit of flesh-eating, but it was known that some had so far approached the ape as to subsist on fruit and vegetables. In the mode of life they had the ape-like custom of crowding together. It was true that when they did so collect they were sufficiently unapelike to destroy all trees and living things and to surround themselves with unnatural noise and light. It must not be forgotten, however, that those in the highest regard (and therefore nearest to the ape) tended not to live in such communities, but to have large separate dwellings in whose neighbourhood the trees and fields were left unmolested. In the matter of marriage customs there were, it was true, wide variations. Some races had the human habit of several wives, or of changing them frequently. On the other hand, many had achieved the monkey state of monogamy. It was unhappily true that they were incapable of intelligent communication. But it was perhaps not too much to suppose that the queer discordant cries that proceeded from their lips when several were in company had some meaning. Finally, he came to their settled habit of exterminating one another for every sort of cause and lack of cause. Here in truth they were least bestial. But could it be urged that the apes never fell to manlike levels in this particular?...

So the formidable argument continued. A hurried Convention of Elders was summoned, at which it was decided, first, to let it be known that this doctrine was damnable heresy, and secondly, to end the danger to the simian world by the execution of the heretic. Both decisions were duly carried out, and both were widely applauded. But it was like the obstinate blasphemy of Bandar to exclaim as they slew him:

"E pur si muove," by which he was understood to mean that in so acting the apes had behaved exactly like men.

THE GAME AND THE CANDLE

"I have invented a new game," said the Spirit of Evil. "Child," said the Spirit of Good, smiling benevolently, "will you never grow up? Ah well, go away and play with it."

"But," said the Spirit of Evil, deeply disappointed, "it won't be any fun unless I tell you about it."

"How long will it take?" inquired the Spirit of Good cautiously.

"Only a million or two years at most," said the Spirit of Evil.

"In that case I will listen. What do you call it, child?"

"I call it man," said the Spirit of Evil, and he described humanity to the Spirit of Good.

"You horrid, disgusting little wretch," said the Spirit of Good after she had listened patiently for a few thousand centuries. "Stop that game at once. I won't have it."

"But, Good darling!" said Evil, "you did enjoy it when they believed that you had invented them, now didn't you?"

"It certainly was funny," said Good with a gentle sigh, "but all the same, I rather blame myself for having listened."

"But it was only a game," said Evil.

"That's true," said Good, "but be more careful with the next one."

ONCE BITTEN, TWICE SHY

When the Last Trumpet had cleared men off the earth like crumbs off a cloth, an unbelievable sweetness and freedom settled over the world. Presently all that man had spoiled was healed, and earth was a garden and God took his pleasure walking in it.

There's a gold apple tree grows in the garden, and if God is so minded of all other trees he plucks the fruit, but at this he holds his hand and muses. The green serpent fawns about his feet. "If thou art God indeed," he whispers, "eat." But God bends and strokes the glittering coils.

"Do thou eat, belovéd," says he, "and be even as I am, having knowledge of good and evil—and of thyself." "Get thou behind me, God," cries the serpent, and is fled through the dust of the garden like a green flame. And when the sweet laughter of God is over, all is quiet in the garden.

XL

IT TAKES TWO TO MAKE A PEACE

After the war, which he believed himself to have won, the everlasting No met, as he was travelling grandly in his great car, his defeated enemy, the everlasting Yes. This second, as became one so heavily defeated, went on foot, in rags, and seemed something of a cripple.

"Ha," said No, "I am sorry to see you in such case, but you will not deny that even so I let you off lightly. I tremble to think what vengeance you would have exacted had you triumphed. Confess that you would have exterminated me and not limited yourself to ruining and crippling me."

"Why," said Yes reflectively, "I stand for acceptance. I have other names, too—Love, Hope and Charity. But as acceptance trails your shadow of refusal, so do my other names trail theirs—Hate, Despair and Unimaginativeness—and the worst of these shadows is unimaginativeness. I had dreamed, I confess, that it would be well to wipe out the shadows."

"As I thought," said No, "for all your specious claims you are harder of heart than I."

"As acceptance," said Yes, "must always be harder than refusal and life than death."

"But," cried No triumphantly, "you were wrong. Here go you in rags for all your lights, and here ride I in purple for all my shadows."

"I was wrong," said Yes, "because I was young. I did not see that I must accept you and your shadows with the rest. I was fighting not against you but against myself when I would not accept as part of myself the great refusal."

"What!" cried No, deeply mortified and inwardly afraid, "beggar that you are, do you dare to claim that you have won?"

"I only know," said Yes gently, "that there is no victory."

"You canting hypocrite," cried No, "you do not know how to take a licking."

"It is because I do," said Yes, "that there cannot be victory or defeat. For if the fight were ended where would you be, where I?"

"There is something in that," said No disconsolately; "but if it be true, why should you fight? Let us make an eternal peace!"

"That would be to refuse," said Yes.

"Damn you," cried No, "I will have peace."

"It takes two," said Yes gently, "to make a peace," and turned to limp away.

"But Yes," cried No after him, now thoroughly dismayed, "how is all this to end?"

"Dear No," said Yes, "it does not end."

XLI

VICISTI GALILÆE

Down a path in the wood she came singing. The path on which she walked was itself like a song under leaves like music. The path was the echo of the song, or the song of the path. It does not matter. This was before music and the world made of music had fallen apart.

His shadow fell on the path. The song stopped; the path grew still.

"It is quiet, quiet," she said.

"It is love," said he.

"Something has died," she whispered.

"And has risen from the dead," he cried, drawing very close. "Love has conquered death."

"Alas," she said, taking his hand and kissing it, "before love came there was no death to conquer."

Humbert Wolfe – A Concise Bibliography

London Sonnets (1920)
Shylock Reasons with Mr. Chesterton and other poems (1920)
"Labour Ministry and Department of Labour (United Kingdom)" and "Labour Supply and Regulation (United Kingdom)" Encyclopedia Britannica, Vol. XXXI (1922)
Circular Saws (1923)
Labour Supply and Regulation (1923)
The Lilac (1924)
Lampoons (1925)
The Unknown Goddess (1925) Poems
Humoresque (1926)
News of the Devil (1926) Poems
Requiem (1927) Poems

Cursory Rhymes (1927) Poems
Others Abide (1927)
Kensington Gardens (1924)
Dialogues and Monologues (1928) Criticism
This Blind Rose (1928) Poems
Troy (1928) Ariel poems
The Moon and Mrs. Misses Smith (1928)
The Craft of Verse (1928) Essay
The Silver Cat and other poems (1928)
Notes on English Verse Satire (1929)
A Winter Miscellany (1930) Editor
Homage to Meleager (1930)
Tennyson (1930)
The Uncelestial City (1930)
Early Poems (1930)
George Moore (1931)
Snow (1931) Poems
Signpost to Poetry (1931)
Reverie of Policeman: A ballet in three acts (1933)
Now a Stranger (1933) Autobiography
Romantic and Unromantic Poetry (1933)
Truffle Eater. Pretty Stories and funny pictures (under the alias 'Oistros' with pictures by Archibald Louis Charles Savory (1933)
Portraits by Inference (1934)
Sonnets pour Helene (by Ronsard) (1934) Translator
X at Oberammergau: A poem (1935) Drama
The Fourth of August (1935) Poems
Selected Lyrics of Heinrich Heine (1935) Translator
P. L. M.: Peoples Landfalls Mountains (1936)
The Pilgrim's Way (1936)
The Silent Knight: A Romantic Comedy in Three Acts (by Eugene Heltai) (1937) Translator
Others Abide: Translated Greek Epigrams (1937)
The Upward Anguish (1938) Autobiography
Out of Great Tribulation (1939) Poems
Kensington Gardens in War-Time (1940) Poems

www.ingramcontent.com/pod-product-compliance
Lightning Source LLC
Chambersburg PA
CBHW021945040426
42448CB00008B/1243